Verbs in Action
Turn Into

Dana Meachen Rau

Marshall Cavendish
Benchmark
New York

The air is cool. The leaves turn orange, yellow, and brown. Summer is turning into fall.

Fall will turn into winter. The *seasons* turn every year.

Turn means to change. Once, you were a little baby.

You turned into a child. Someday, you will turn into a grown-up.

A turn in the weather means
that the weather changes.
A sunny day can turn rainy.
Your soccer game might get
canceled.

A rainy day can turn sunny. You can still have your backyard picnic.

Day turns into night because the Earth is turning. The side of the Earth facing the Sun has daytime.

On the side facing away from the Sun, it is night. As the Earth turns, the places with day and night change.

Turning can mean to spin in a circle.

A merry-go-round and a Ferris
wheel turn around and around.
So do the wheels on a bicycle.

Watch the hands on a clock. The long hand turns to mark a minute. The short hand turns to point to the hour.

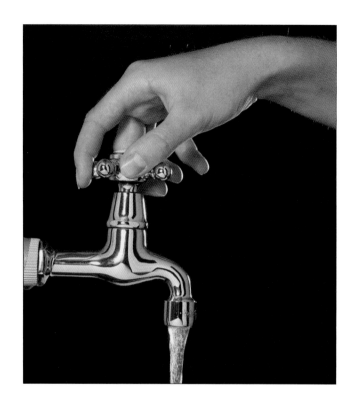

You turn a part on a machine to make it work. You turn the handle on a sink to make the water run.

You turn a doorknob to open a
door. You turn a page to read
this book.

Turning can mean to change *direction*. A road through the mountains might have twists and turns. Your mom has to turn the *steering wheel* a lot.

On a path in the woods, you might need to make a choice. Should you turn right or should you turn left?

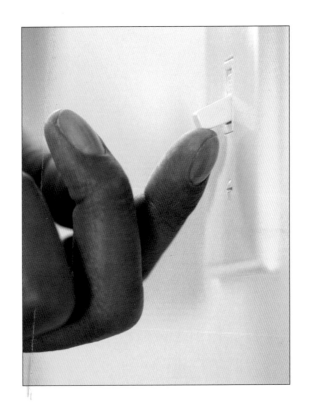

You need light to see in a dark room. Use the *switch* to turn on the light. Now it is bright.

Turn off the light with the switch.
Now it is dark and hard to see.

In spring, people "turn over" their gardens. They turn over the dirt with a shovel so that fresh soil is on top. Then they plant seeds. The seeds will turn into plants.

The *bleachers* are packed.
You might say a lot of people
"turned out" for the big game.

The crowd watches the players
take turns at bat.

Have you ever lost one of your socks? You look everywhere. Do not worry. Your sock will "turn up" soon.

If you are sad, you might "turn to" a friend to cheer you up.

Day is turning into night. Now it is time to "turn in." You need to get lots of sleep. Tomorrow might turn into a busy day!

Challenge Words

bleachers (BLEECH-uhrz)—The benches at sporting events that people sit on.

direction (duhr-EK-shuhn)—The way something is moving or facing.

seasons (SEE-zuhns)—Times of the year with very different weather.

steering wheel—The part of a car that people turn to change direction.

switch—A simple device that turns things on and off.

Index

Page numbers in **boldface** are illustrations.

With thanks to Nanci Vargus, Ed.D.
and Beth Walker Gambro, reading consultants

Marshall Cavendish Benchmark
Marshall Cavendish
99 White Plains Road
Tarrytown, New York 10591-9001
www.marshallcavendish.us

Library of Congress Cataloging-in-Publication Data

Rau, Dana Meachen, 1971-
Turn into / by Dana Meachen Rau.
p. cm. — (Bookworms. Verbs in action)
Summary: "Discusses the action described by a verb, while making connections between people and other living and nonliving objects. It also talks about other uses of the word in commonly used phrases."
—Provided by publisher.
Includes index.
ISBN-13: 978-0-7614-2293-8
ISBN-10: 0-7614-2293-5
1. Turn (The English word)—Juvenile literature. 2. English language—Verb—Juvenile literature. I. Title. II. Series.
PE1317.T87R38 2006
428.1—dc22
2005026783

Photo Research by Anne Burns Images

Cover Photo by Corbis/Grace/zefa

The photographs in this book are used with permission and through the courtesy of:
Corbis: pp. 1, 10 Gabe Palmer; p. 2 Claude Woodruff; p. 3 Ariel Skelley; p. 4 Owen Franken; pp. 5, 6 Randy Faris; p. 7 Philip James Corwin; p. 9 Janis Miglavs; p. 11 Richard Cummins; p. 12 Wolfgang Flamisch; p. 17 Conrad Zobel; pp. 18, 20 Royalty Free; p. 21 Joe Bator; p. 23 Lynda Richardson; p. 24 William Manning; p. 25 Tom & Dee Ann McCarthy. *Photo Researchers, Inc.*: p. 8 Roger Haris. *SuperStock*: p. 14 SuperStock; p. 15 ThinkStock; p. 27 Neal & Molly Jansen; p. 29 BananaStock.

Printed in Malaysia
1   3   5   6   4   2